GUARDIANS OF SPITI VALLEY

SOCIAL INEQUALITY AND RESOURCE MANAGEMENT

ARSHAQ HABIB

Firstly I would like to thank my parents and family members for all the support. I am grateful to Dr. Wajeeda Bano, Economics Department and Dr. A M Khan for the encouragement. In particular I would like to thank my PhD supervisor Dr. Mustiary Begum at Mangalore University, Dr. Joseph PD, Coordinator of MBA (Tourism and Travel Management) Mangalore University, Prof Shekar Naik, Associate Professor of MBA (Tourism and Travel Management), Dr Jagath Thimmaiah, Principal of FMKMC college, Prof Rangappa, Coordinator of Tourism and travel management for all the support. I would like to thank my best friend Prof. Noushad H, Assistant Professor at Government First Grade College Mudigere. I wish to place my gratitude to my colleagues and students of Field Marshal KM Cariappa College who have contributed directly or indirectly in the making of this book. Sincere thanks to my sister Fathima Afreen for editing and correcting this book.Sincere thanks to Mrs. Sowmya SN. I would also like to thank Shameer SR for the guidance and the designing of this book.

Contents

Acknowledgements

Special thanks to people of Himachal Pradesh.

I
INTRODUCTION

Key Monestry

Spiti Valley is located in the present day Indian state of Himachal Pradesh. Currently, it has a population of around 12,000 people living in a 7,100 sq. km.25 territory. Geographically, it is situated in the rain shadow of the

Himalayas, which deprives the valley of the Indian monsoon rains. Spiti's extreme altitude (many villages in Spiti are situated higher than 4,000 meters above sea level, with the lowest villages in Spiti being over 3000m above sea level) and arid landscape distinguishes Spiti and its neighboring region of upper Kinnaur from other regions of Himachal Pradesh.

Partly due to its high and arid geographical conditions, Spiti is relatively isolated. Most tourists as well as anthropological researchers visiting the region choose to visit the neighboring region of Ladakh, which has similar cultural and geographical environments but is connected by an airport facility and better road infrastructure - and thus a stronger tourist economy. The road connecting Spiti to the nearest Indian town of Manali, much of which is unpaved, is normally closed from November to April every year due to snow.

The 1962 border war between India and China resulted in Spiti, along with its neighboring region of Ladakh, being closed to tourists and Indians from outside the region. While Ladakh was opened to tourists in 1974, Spiti was kept off-limits to tourists,as well as to non-local Indians, until 1993. The opening of Ladakh attracted substantial anthropological research in the region. In recent decades, research in Ladakh has continued, and includes a dedicated international association of scholars and even a Ladakh Studies journal. In contrast, very little anthropological and sociological research has been carried out in Spiti (exceptions include Jahoda, 2007, 2008; and Dollfus, 2004). The most detailed academic research related to Spiti's history and culture has been done in the field of Buddhist Studies, mainly through the study of Buddhist art, architecture, and manuscripts found in its ancient temples and monasteries.

Spiti is most well-known for its old Buddhist temples and monasteries. These sites have attracted some of the pioneer scholars of Tibetan Buddhism (Tucci, 1935/1988;1957/1995) and continue to draw researchers to Spiti (Klimburg-Salter, 1997; ropper, 2008). Several of Spiti's temples and monasteries are believed to be more than a thousand years old. During the 10th century, the Buddhist rulers of the newly founded Guge kingdom supported the Great Translator Rinchen Zangpo (lo tsa ba chen po rin chen bzang po) in a project whose objective was to translate all the major Sanskrit Buddhist texts into the Tibetan language and to build temples, monasteries and stupas in the region (mainly Ladakh, Zanskar, Spiti, Upper Kinnaur, Guge and Purang).

These initiatives also promoted significant cultural and scholarly exchanges between Tibetan and Indian scholars and artists (Klimburg-Salter, 1997), as evidenced by standardized Tibetan translations of Sanskrit Buddhist texts from this time as well as by the Indian (Kashmiri) influenced art and iconography featured in the Buddhist temples of the Alchi Monastery in Ladakh and the Tabo Monastery in Spiti. Spiti was a key site of these initiatives (Klimburg-Salter, 1997; Tucci, 1935/1988),27 which laid the foundation for what is known in Tibetan Buddhist historiography as the "Second Diffusion of Buddhism".28 The legacy of this period is such that even today Spiti and its neighboring regions (including Ladakh in the Indian state of Jammu and Kashmir, Lahaul and upper Kinnaur in Himachal Pradesh, and the Ngari region of Tibet) share many aspects of religious culture, social customs, institutions, belief systems, and language.

The main features found in all these regions are the dominance of Tibetan Buddhism in all aspects of life, belief in mountain deities and serpent spirits, and agriculture as the economic mainstay of the people.Local notions of gender and gender roles in Spiti are also similar to those in the Tibetan-speaking regions of the Himalayas (Gyatso, 1987; Huber, 1994; Tsomo, 2004). While Spiti shares its high altitude mountainous desert landscape and Tibetan Buddhist culture with its Tibetan and Ladakhi neighboring regions, it also has distinct cultural and socio-economic characteristics. Some of these distinct attributes are a product of more

recent history, while others are more ancient. Among Spiti's distinct cultural features with ancient roots are its local dialect and calendar system. Although people in Spiti speak a Western Tibetan dialect, an Indian linguist who has compiled a substantial dictionary of Spiti words (Mathews, personal communication, May 6, 2011) mentioned that the Spiti dialect – with its own local variations – has its own distinctive linguistic characteristics that are not found in the Ladakhi and central Tibetan languages.30 Perhaps a more noteworthy and relevant cultural feature of Spiti is that Spiti has a unique system of timekeeping, with the names of the months of the calendar being based on ecological, seasonal and agricultural cycle. Compared to both the Tibetan and Ladakhi systems, this calendar system is unique in terms of the timing of the year cycle (including the timing of the new year)32 and the names of the months (Gergan,1978).As indicated from Spiti's naming of the months according to agricultural seasons,trade and pastoralism. Today, the government also plays a central role by employing a significant number of the adult population as road construction workers, teachers, nurses, and bureaucrats, as well as in a host of other capacities. Therefore, although I use the word "farmer" to generically describe the people of Spiti in this study, it must be pointed out that today people are engaged in a host of livelihood (income) sources in addition to their common occupation of farming. For example, the father of my host family is a local

doctor, a farmer and a proficient local architect, all of which are closely tied to activities in the village. At the same time, he also works as an employee of the state government as a forest guard. In addition, during the four years when I was engaged in my fieldwork, he started and completed building a large four-story house, which he plans to run as a guesthouse for tourists.

Social stratification and socio-economic structure of Spiti Valley Literature on social stratification in Tibetan (Carrasco, 1959; Goldstein, 1971; Aziz, 1978; Wiley, 1986), Ladakhi (Crook, 1994) and Spiti (Jahoda, 2008) societies shows similarities in socio-economic class structure, albeit with minor regional and local differences. Households with farming land and irrigation rights, with associated tax obligations, form the basic corporate entities of the Tibetan socio-economic system. A Tibetan village is typically comprised of several classes of households. These are, starting from the top: aristocrats, tantric practitioners (Joba or Ngagpa), Tibetan medicine practitioners (Amchi), taxpayer farmers, landless Dhutul (or Dhuchung) farmers, and outcastes. The minor differences at the regional and local level are mainly demonstrated in the compositions of different classes of people or households.

Some regions and villages within a region have a greater percentage of one particular class of households, while others have less or none of these households. For example, the outcaste group of Beda, which is present in the western Himalayan regions of Ladakh and Spiti is absent in central Tibet. An example of differences in class structure within a region would be the fact that many villages in Spiti have only two kinds of households (i.e., Khangchen and Dhutul), while many others have three kinds of households (i.e., Khangchen, Dhutul and outcastes). These kinds of differences are further outlined in the chart below, which compares the social stratifications characteristic of Tibet and Spiti. The percentage of aristocrats in Spiti Valley (only one household)34 is significantly lower than that of Tibet.

Another important difference is that Spiti has only two types of outcaste households (i.e., blacksmiths and musicians), whereas Tibet has several types of outcastes.

II

Khangchen households

Locals believe that Khangchen households are the founders and the oldest households of the village.35 That is why these households are also referred to as the "Old Households" (khang chen rnying pa). These households were also called "tax payers" (khral pa) because only this group of households was historically responsible for paying taxes to the ruler.36 The farming estates of these households formed the basic unit of agricultural production and taxation which constituted the traditional economy. As tax-payers, thesehouseholds (i.e., the men of these households) had legal rights to all of the arable land and irrigation sources of the village. These men also represented the Village Council and hence were the decision makers; they thus constituted the most powerful group of households in the village. How did the Khangchen households come to own all the local resources and decisionmaking powers, and how does the Khangchen household system perpetuate this arrangement? According to common belief, the Khangchen households have privileged ownership over all farming land and irrigation water because they are (or are believed to be) the male descendants of the oldest households of the village.

Locals believe that there were a total of 250 such households in the beginning, which were known as the "250 soldiers"38 (Interviews, 2010, 2011). The old Khangchen households of today thusrepresent the descendants of the 250 soldiers. Local elders mentioned that these 250 Khangchen households still exist and that the number has not changed much in history, if at all.Maintaining the continuity in the number and size of land holdings was an important characteristic of the Khangchen household system (Wylie, 1986, p. 6). This continuity is maintained by a system of primogeniture, whereby the property is passed on to the eldest son when he gets married. This practice continues from one generation to the next, with local laws existing to ensure that the property is not divided into smaller pieces. For example, while it is customary to give small pieces of land of Khangchen property to support certain family members, such as a monk brother (who is given a "monk field" or dra zhing) or elder parents, these pieces of land must be returned to the Khangchen household after the death of the family members to whom these were given.

Dhutul households

Dhutul households are generally described as those "who have nothing but a house, being literally a smoke-maker" (Gazetteer, 1883, p. 439). Members of Dhutul households were traditionally landless farmers who were dependent on Khangchen households for work (Lyall, 1874, p. 185).40 Although this class of household is socio-economically weaker than the Khangchen, members of both Dhutul and Khangchen households are considered qually pure, and known as Yarab ("good manners"), as opposed to the ritually impure members of caste households, who are known as Marab ("vulgar"/"immoral").The Dhutul class of farmers comprises the majority of the Spiti population.

According to local history, in the beginning, there were 600 "Za" or Dhutul households along with the250 "soldier" or Khangchen households. Other historical data on Dhutuls is generally not available. That this group of households did not pay taxes to the ruler is probably why the British did not seek to provide census figures specific to this category. The Indian Government does not differentiate between Khangchen and Dhutul households because both categories (as well as everyone else in Spiti) have been exempted from taxation.

Jahoda (2008) has shown that the number of Dhutul farmers has increased significantly since Spiti became a part of India, which is consistent with my field observations. The total population of Spiti has increased from 4,222 in 1951 (a figure based on independent India's first national census) to 11,852 in 2010 (a figure based on the last national census). Given that the total number of Khangchen households has changed very little (as mentioned above) and since the caste population makes up only a small section of the local population (5.6%, according to the 2001 census), we can deduce that the number of Dhutul households has increased the most over the last few decades. This is consistent with studies done by Jahoda (2008) on demographic changes in Spiti's Tabo village, which show that the majority of the increase in population belongs to the Dhutul category, formed mainly through the fissioning of Old Khangchen and Dhutul households.

The main factor that made the increase in population socio-economically feasible was the 1968 Nautor land grant program (discussed below). After this program was introduced, all of the landless households in Zibug and Khyung villages were given land, which made it possible for many of them to formally enter the ranks of the Khangchen class by paying "full" village taxes. Thus, the socio-economic status or power of the Dhutul households rose significantly after the passage of the Himachal Pradesh Nautor Land Rules act of 1968.

"Caste" or Marab households

At the bottom of the village social structure are the two outcaste Marab households: Zo blacksmiths and Beda musicians. It is unknown when and how Zo households came to Spiti but the Beda were introduced under Ladakhi rule (discussed below). Today, Zo and Beda households are more commonly known – in local speech and government records, as well as in academic publications – as "caste" or "Scheduled Caste" households. During my field research, I observed that farmers use the word "caste" more often than "Marab", even while speaking in the local language.

The use of the term "caste" to refer to these two groups of households in Spiti is also standard in academic publications (e.g., Mishra et al., 2003; Gutschow, 2006; Jahoda 2007 & 2008; Tsering & Ishimura, 2012), where it is normally clarified or implicitly assumed that the term specifically refers to local outcaste groups and does not concern the Indian caste organization. This study will also use the term "caste" to refer to Zo

and/or Beda households/members; this is not to imply, however, that the system is thesame as the Hindu caste system. Here I want to emphasize that the uncritical use of the term "caste" can reify caste biases. Although an option to avoid such reification is to not use the term, I chose to actively use it because this study directly concerns socioeconomicinequities experienced by Zo and Beda members precisely because of their outcaste status, which is more strongly expressed by the term "caste" than "marab." Moreimportantly, I believe that the reification of caste inequities happens when the term is used in an uncritical manner. This study, on the contrary, reveals and critically analyzes routine discrimination experienced by outcaste members in the domains of farming and resource management. The social beliefs and practices concerning caste members in Spiti are similar to those concerning outcastes in Tibet (Carrasco, 1959; Aziz, 1978; Gombo, 1983; Childs, 2003) and other Himalayan Buddhist regions such as Ladakh (Rather, 1997) and Khumbu in Nepal (Ortner, 1973). In addition to lower social status, caste members are believed to be irreversibly defiled - according to local notions of purity. Members of Chechang households follow two main rules of exclusion against caste members: prohibition on marital relations and on sharing the same drinking cup. In the rare cases of marital relations or "mixing of mouths" between Chechang and caste members, the result is that the Chechang person involved permanently loses his or her status. Finally, it must benoted here that, in Spiti, caste is a stronger determinant of a person's status than is gender.

Spiti has a relatively coherent historical narrative from the 10th century onwards (Lahuli, 2002). Before the 10th century, the only thing generally known or accepted in Hindi (e.g., Sankrityayan, 1948/2006, 1994, 2002), Tibetan (e.g., mkhas pa'i dga' ston; Gyalpo, 2006; Shastri, 2007) and English (e.g., Thakur, 2000; Petech, 1997) language sources is that Spiti once formed a part of the Zhangzhung kingdom (periodization unknown). This seems to have been the case until the region became a part of an expanding Tibetan Empire sometime in the mid 7th century (Sankrityayan, 1994, 2002).

A major contribution of this chapter is the original hypothesis presented which answers the question raised at the beginning - that regarding the historical origin and legal basis of the Khangchen household's privileged access to local farming lands and irrigationsources. Drawing on ancient Tibetan texts, studies based on original source materials from the time of the Tibetan Empire and local oral history, as well as my own field research, I hypothesized that Spiti's Khangchen system of taxation, which is directly associated with the privileges enjoyed by Khangchen households in terms of access rights to farming lands and irrigation sources, is based on the military administrative system of the Tibetan Empire that was established between the 7th-9th centuries A.D. This hypothesis is highly relevant for this study - not only because it provides a definite historical period and context for understanding the privileged powers of the contemporary Khangchen households but also for the light that it sheds on the origin of Spiti's most prominent class of household. After the collapse of the Tibetan Empire, the next major power that introduced important changes in local culture was the kingdom of Guge. Starting in the 10th century, the rulers of the Guge kingdom supported an active missionary campaign to introduce and establish Buddhism in the region, mainly through the construction of temples and monasteries, as well as through the translation of Sanskrit Buddhist texts into the Tibetan language. Spiti was an important site of these activities partly because it was located between the Guge kingdom and Kashmir. Kashmir was a center of Buddhist activity at that time, and a key source of Buddhist knowledge for the Guge kingdom. In addition to introducing Buddhism, the Guge kingdom also established monasteries in Spiti, and by implication, introduced the Monastic Estates taxation system. Guge was followed by the kingdom of Ladakh, which introduced the institution of the Nono, the local administrative ruler, who in turn introduced the Beda musicians into Spiti.While all the classes of households in the hierarchical village social structure – Khangchen, Dhutul and caste – were established by the time the British took over Spiti in 1846, British laws resulted in rendering the dominant Khangchen households more powerful, thereby weakening the traditionally underprivileged groups (such as women and members of caste and Dhutul households). Under the previous Ladakhi and Tibetan legal systems, although Khangchen men normally enjoyed full rights over their estates, they were in fact legal tenants, as all land belonged to the state. British laws privatized land ownership, making the Khangchen men registered owners of their estates. In addition, the British also documented and legalized local customs, including those related to the management of resources such as irrigation, fodder and firewood. These measures provided lasting legal protection for ancient customs that privileged certain members of society over others.

These customs were and still are highly inequitable because the privileged group of Khangchen men are a small minority compared to the rest of the village population, which is composed of women, children and elders as wellas members of Dhutul and caste households. As discussed in the following chapters, these codified customs, in the form of government administrative papers, are still valid and continue to affect local farming and resource management customs. Spiti saw the greatest changes, both in terms of material economic conditions and in terms of local power relations, under the rule of the current Indian State. These changes, which are still unfolding, are a result of the Indian initiative aimed at developing and integrating the local economy and administration with the larger Indian economy and administration. Certain policies have been implemented through significant economic investments and a variety of administrative measures introduced to consolidate statecontrol over Spiti, which, since the 1962 India-China war, has been recognized as a sensitive border region. In terms of the impact on local power relations, these socioeconomic development initiatives are being received favorably by the people, particularly by the underprivileged sections of the society, who often refer to the Indian government as "kind and gracious". For the first time in history, women and members of Dhutul and caste households are not only able to own land and engage in commercial agriculture, but they are also able to acquire free education and get jobs in the service economy. However, the impact of the development initiatives on different sections of society are more complex and uneven than meets the eye. For example, the men of the Khangchen and Dhutul households have been able to take greater advantage of the opportunities provided by the state than men of caste households and women in general. Therefore, despite dramatic changes over the course of recent decades, the hierarchical social relations of power still persist, especially in the customary practices involving farming and resource management.

III

Inequalities Within Women-Managed Irrigation Systems

Localites of Spiti Valley

Intersectional theory argues that although gender has powerful outcomes on people's lives, it does not operate alone. Gender always operates in relation to other social differences such as race, class, caste and ethnicity and this in turn results in amultilayered system of disadvantage for some people and privilege for others. For example, in Canadian society, it can be said that aboriginal and black women from lowincome households face multiple dimensions of disadvantage (of race, ethnicity and class) as compared to, for example, a white middle-class women. Therefore, intersectional approaches analyze the interplay of gender and other social differences and seek to unravel and shed light upon how certain groups are multiply disadvantaged while others are privileged. In this sense, the application of intersectional analysis to water management issues posits that although sex-gender based inequities around water issues are important, this alone is not sufficient to understand and address issues of inequity because sex-gender is only one of the many important intersecting layers of social relations that mediate different gendered water relations. Specifically, it has been pointed out that the intersection between gender and socio-economic class (Sultana et al., 2013) or poverty (Harris, 2008) is an important area for analysis and theorization. Validating these arguments, this chapter unravels intersectional differences among different groups of women, as contrasted with a men-versus-women approach, in terms of their socioeconomic class and caste backgrounds.

This case study, which examines the inequality among women groups is significant in some ways. First, "too often, inequalities among women are overlooked in initiatives romoting women's rights and interests" (Sultana et al., 2013, p. 13). This is true in general and for irrigation management in particular. Second, as the description of local irrigation activities in this chapter demonstrates, women are responsible for almost all of these activities. This is in contrast to the situation portrayed in the larger literature -which generally assumes women's secondary status based on exclusion from irrigation practices. In Spiti, irrigation is the domain of women. However it is nonetheless the case that important processes of social differentiation and inequalities operate through their engagement and are reinforced by it, as well as being additionally reinforced through state practices.

This chapter is composed of three main sections. The first section provides relevant historical and geographical contexts that form the basis of some of the main features of the social organization of Spiti's irrigation system. The second section provides a translation and analysis of the text of codified irrigation customs of Zibug and Kyung villages in Spiti Valley. I pay attention to the historical context in which the irrigation customs were codified in order to shed light on the nature of the language of the legal text and its impact on local power relations. I also analyze how unequal power relations in access to and management of irrigation water in terms of gender and landholdings are cemented in law. The third section, presented in order to highlight the inequalities and internal politics embedded in these activities, provides a detailed ethnographicdescription of irrigation-related activities performed by farmers (these practices are similar in both the villages) according to their ascribed gender, class and caste roles. The description of irrigation activities shows that women perform almost all of these activities. From an intersectional perspective, gender is unique because it exists in not only every household (Agarwal, 2007) but also in every socio-economic class, with each class often having a different set of expected roles. That is why one should not lump all women into one group and simply say that women perform irrigation-related tasks. Instead, one

should analyze which categories of women perform which kinds of irrigation-related tasks; this is due to the fact that these tasks can be seen as hierarchical based on the ascribed roles of women belonging to different household types. In addition, inspired by Ribot and Peluso's (2003) suggestions on empirically observing the differences between ability and right to benefit from things in understanding access to property, I analyze gender equity not only based on empirical observations of "who performs which irrigation tasks" but also on an analysis of "who are excluded and why". I show how an analysis on exclusion, particularly covert exclusionary practices, can yield insights into deeper layers of micro-politics between different groups.

Irrigation system of Spiti Valley and its social organization

Kelly (1983) has noted that the "widely used concept of an 'irrigation system' typically conflates three distinct dimensions of agricultural water use: natural water flow patterns, hysical networks of facilities and environmental modifications, and organization of configurations of irrigation roles" (pp. 880-881). It is therefore important to emphasizethat this study is only concerned with the social organization of irrigation management.Another analytical aspect of the study that must be clarified at the outset is that it is concerned only with irrigation systems related to old fields that are located next to the village. Generally, there are three main types of fields in Spiti: village fields, mountainfields, and Nautor fields. Village fields are the traditional or historical fields that are situated in and around the immediate vicinity of a village. These are the fields to which all irrigation and farming-related customary laws apply. Mountain fields (ri zhing) are located a few kilometers away from the village and are cultivated by one or a few villagers. Although farmers of mountain fields irrigate and cultivate their fields according to customs, they are not obligated to follow every custom. Finally, Nautor fields are those that were allocated by the Indian government to landless and poor farmers after the passage of the Nautor Land Rules Act. Nautor fields are located several kilometers away from most of the villages, including Zibug and Khyung.Though Zibug and Khyung farmers own all three kinds of fields, this study is concerned only with the historical village fields. I have focused on the historical village fields because farmers' work on these fields is regulated by stringent traditional customs. In the mountain fields and Nautor fields, farmers are not required to follow all the traditional customs. Thus irrigation practices in the historical village fields, even though these are performed in a contemporary context, can nevertheless be considered "traditional" practices. In addition, the codified irrigation customs of Zibug and Khyung villages, which are translated and analyzed below, only concern the village fields. Another advantage of focusing on village fields is that these are representative of the village. Mountain fields are not the ideal sites for a study of village customs because these fields are like a family compound, belonging to only one or a small group of households. Nautor fields are not only recent creations and situated far away from the villages but are composed of fields belonging to farmers of many different villages.Technically, as we shall see below, there are only two groups of irrigation users in the village fields: Khangchen households (representing one group) and members from the rest of village (lumped together and composing the second group). In terms of numbers, Khangchen households are the minority but they have most of the rights over irrigation water. Although the second group, comprised of Dhutul and caste households, are numerically much larger (numbers discussed below), they have very limited access to irrigation water. Other key features of the social organization of Spiti's irrigation system include:

1) Men of Khangchen households are the legal rights holders of irrigation water and they thus make most of the key decisions, such as the commencement timing regarding different irrigation activities;

2) Women do most of the irrigation-related work; and

3) Many women from Dhutul and caste households work as Chu pa (irrigators) for Khangchen households on a contractual basis. These features are explained in more detail in their historical and geographical contexts in the next section.

Another important factor that further explains why only women perform irrigation work in Spiti is its geographical and environmental contexts. Owing to its geographical location in the high Himalayas (both Zibug and Khyung villages are situated slightly higher than 4000 meters above sea level), Spiti has a short growing season and long snowy winters. Owing to these conditions, every household must collect a large enough stock of firewood and dung to ensure that their heating and cooking needs will be met throughout the long winter months. The small villages of Spiti are scattered along the river valley and each village has a relatively large commons areas within which farmers collect firewood and dung.93 Collection of firewood is a relatively challenging task, which, for various reasons (discussed in chapter 6), local custom has reserved only for men. One of the reasons is the physical difficulty of the task. The main sources of firewood are two thorny shrubs, Caragana versicolor (gra ma) and Lonicera (brab), which both grow in the highest and driest areas. The thorny shrubs are mainly uprooted with the hands, using brute physical force, and with the help of adze hoes. In addition, farmers must travel long distances with yaks to carry the collected firewood. The collection of firewood (and dung) from distant mountainous areas as an exclusive livelihood role of men has had direct implications for irrigation being the exclusive livelihood role of women. As mentioned earlier, farm work (except for activities thatrequire the use of yaks for plowing and threshing crops) is mainly done by women.

During the short summer months, men have to go to the mountains regularly to collect (and stock) firewood, which leaves only women to do the irrigation work. The division of labor therefore had to be based on gender, as opposed to age, because both irrigation and the collection of firewood has to be regularly done by healthy adults as these tasks require skilled experience, as well as physical strength and endurance.

IV

Gender, agrarian socio-economic class and farming labor

In the previous chapter, I showed how women do most of the irrigation work based on their class and caste roles. That irrigation is largely the domain of women raises an important question about gender power relations: is the custom of women doing irrigation-related work a manifestation of society's oppression of women? This possibility was indeed suggested in some of the interviews with farmers. When asked why only women do irrigation and farming work and men do not help, farmers (mostly women farmers) simply say that this has been the local social custom. In this chapter, I will show that women's irrigation role is part of a broader division of agricultural labor which is based on gender. Just as irrigation is the domain of women, there are other farming-related activities, such as plowing and the reading of ritual scriptures, that aredone only by men. This chapter will show that the number of agriculture-related tasks done by men is more or less the same as those done by women. However, this does not mean that there is gender equity in agricultural labor. As was the case in the

previous chapter, this chapter will take a more complex approach to equity by undertaking an intersectional analysis of gender and socio-economic class in farming-related activities.

To better understand the micropolitics of agricultural labor roles, I argue that there is a need for better theorizing around the role of the desirability or prestige associated with different tasks and the role of exclusion of underprivileged or weaker groups (especially in ritual-related activities).

While tasks that are considered sinful are done by women or men of caste households, the meritorious or virtuous farming roles, especially those that require specialized knowledge such as the ability to do astrological calculation or perform religious rituals, are done by non-caste men, mostly of Khangchen backgrounds. The performance of these ritual activities is considered fundamental and meritorious because, from the perspective of the farmers, these activities relate to the most sacred and powerful forces that affect theirlivelihood. Farmers strongly believe in the existence of local deities, serpent spirits and other divine beings that must be appeased ritually so that these powerful beings will support the farmers' livelihood. For example, farmers believe that the village lands belong to a local deity or deities first, which is clearly articulated in the local term for these deities: "owner of the lands" (gzhi bdag). Therefore, getting approval and blessings from these deities is considered necessary for all farming activities that must be performed on the deity's land. Similarly, as pointed out in the previous chapter, villagers believe in serpent spirits, which they say are sensitive beings that control the water sources as well as the climate. Appeasement of these serpent spirits is thus also necessary to ensure adequate rain as well as a reliable supply of water in the mountain springs. The rituals for deity and serpent spirit propitiation are, however, technical religious activities that require specialized knowledge as well as the ability to read scriptures.

V

Conclusion

Our Visit to Spiti

Evidence from these case studies points to the need to go beyond general approaches to gender and equity in irrigation management. In the current literature on irrigation management, equity is generally theorized along an enquiry as to whether the fields get water with equal frequency and whether the allocation of water is proportional to the size of the fields (Trawick, 2001, 2003). This study shows that these two features are not sufficient to assess whether an irrigation system is truly equitable as these case studies satisfy these features but also have, for example, a small minority of farmers owning the majority of the fields and the water rights, while a vast majority of farmers have only negligible rights. In addition, these case studies highlight unequal decision-making powers and division of irrigation management roles in terms of gender and markers of social differences such as socio-economic class and gender. Moreover, in terms of theoretical approaches to gender and water, past approaches have mostly focused on "men versus women" issues as they are related to power relations in water use, access and management. While it is widely acknowledged that sex-gender is only one of the many intersecting determinants of social difference, any in-depth analysis of the multiple intersectionalities relating to water and gender issues is rare (Harris, 2008). These case studies from the Himalayan region of the Spiti Valley raise questions about general notions of irrigation management roles as they are dominated by men. The case studies show that in certain historical and geographical contexts, it is possible to find cases where women do most of the irrigation-related tasks. Although the discussion in this chapter does not shed light on why irrigation is the exclusive domain of women in Spiti, it doeshighlight a need for a "within-different-groups-of-women" approach to intersectional studies of gender and equity in irrigation management.

Spiti, however, it must be noted that one's household or class/ caste background primarily determines these roles and relationships. Consequently, the other main determinant of farmers' identity, that is, gender role, is determined by one's household type or one's class and caste background. This is the case in all farming-related activities.gender difference in terms of the number of roles is not significant. However, if we consider who performs the relatively more desirable farming roles, we find that men, particularly Khangchen men, perform most of these activities.Women of the lowest social status in Spiti do the least amount of farming but they play an important part in farming-related rituals and festivals by playing music for these events.Similarly, their cooperation in playing music for the village is completely nonvoluntary in nature as they perform out of a sense of fear of the village deity.

References

Bailey, F.G. 1960. Tribe, Caste and Nation. Monchester.
Bandyopadhyay, J., Jayal, N.D., Schoettli, U. and Singh, Chhatrapati, 1985. India's
Environment: Crises and Responses. NatraJ Publishers, Dehra Dun U.P., India.
Barnes, George Camek, Report on the Settlement in the District of Kangra in the
Trans-Sutlej States (Lahore, 1855).
Berreman, Gerald D. 1972. Hindus of the Himalayas: Ethnography and Change,
London, California.
Bidney, David 1953b Theoretical Anthropology. New York; Colombia Univ. Press.
Bierstadt, Robert, 1950. An analysis of social power, American Sociological Review, 15.
Bose, N.K., Some Indian Tribes (Delhi, 1973).
Brookfield, H.C., 1964. The ecology of highland settlement: some suggestions, American Anthropologist, vol.66, no.4, part 2.
Brunzel, Ruth, I 938. The economic organization of primitive peoples, General
Anthropology. Fmaz Boas, ed. New York, Heath.
Calvert, H., "Notes on the Customs and Beliefs m Spiti," Indian Antiquary, XXXVIII, 1909.
Cassirer, Ernst 1956 An Essay on Man: An Introduction to a Philosophy of Human
Culture. New heaven: Yale Univ. Press.
242
Census of India 1961: Village Survey Monographs of Punjab: Tandi - A Village in
Lahaul & Spiti District of Punjab.
Centre for Science and Environment, 1985. The State of India's Environment 1984-
85: The Second Citizen's Report, New Delhi.
Centre for Science and Environment, 1982, The State of India's Environment: ·The

First citizen's Report, New Delhi.
Chandra Kanta, "Lahaul Spiti Ke Lok Jivan Ki Ak Jhalak," Somsi, 6-7 May-July, 1976.
Chaney, E. 1988. Subsistence Projects for Rural Women. In Dankelman, I. and Davidson, J., Women and Environment in the Third World: Alliance for the Future. Earthscan Publications, London.
Chi1de, V. Gordon, 1951. Social Evolution. New York: Schumann.
Clarke, G. 1954. Elements of Ecology, New York, John Wiley.
Conz, E. 1957. Budhism: Its essence and development, Oxford University Press.
Cook, S.F., 1946. Human sacrifice and warfare as factors in the demography of precolonial
Mexico, Human Biology, 18.
Cunningham, Alexander, Ladakh: Physical, Statistical and Historical with Notes of
Surrounding Countires (London, 1854).
Diack, A.H., Final Report on the Revised Settlement of Kulu Sub-division of the
Kangra District 1891 (Lahore, 1898).
Diack, A.H., Gazetteer of the Kangra District Part 11 to IV, Kulu, Lahaul Spiti (Lahore, 1897).
243
Durkheim, Emile 1950 The Rules of Sodological Method. 8th ed. Translated by Sarah A. Solovay and John H. Muller, and edited by George E. G. Catlin, Glencoe, III.: Free Press.
Eckholm, E., 1975. The deterioration of mountain environments. Science, 189.
Eliot, T.S. (1948) 1949. Notes Towards the Definition of Culture. 4.
Evans-Pritchard, E.E. 1965. Witchcraft, Oracles and Magic Among the Azande,
Oxford: Clarendon.
Evans-Pritchard, E. E. 1956. Social Anthropology. London: Cohen & West; Glencoe,
III.
Fallers, Lloyd A. 1956. Bantu Bureaucracy: A Study of Integration and Conflict in
the Political Institutions of an East African People. Cambridge: Heffer.
Firth, Raymond, W. (editor) 1964 Man and Culture: An Evaluation of the

Work of
Bronislaw Malinwski. New York; Happer.
Firth, Raymond W. (ed.) 1964. Man and Culture: An Evaluation of the Work of
Bronislaw Malinowski, New York: Harper.
Firth, Raymong W. 1959 Social Change in Tikopia: Re-study of a Polynesian Community After a Generation. New York: Macmillian; London: Allen & Unwin.
Firth, Raymond, 1929. Primitive Economics of the New Zealand Maori, London,
Routledge.
-Fisher, James F. 1986. Trans-Himalayan Traders: Economy, Society and Culture in
Northwest Nepal. University of California Press, B-erkeley, USA.
Flog, F. and D.G. Bates, 1976. Cultural Anthropology, New York.
244
Fortes, Meyer 1955 Radcliffe-Brown's Contributions to the study of Social Organization British Journal of Sociology 6:
Frake, Charles, 0., 1962. Cultural ecology and ehtnography, American Anthropologist, 64.
Geertz, C. 1959. Form and Variation m Balinese Village Structure. American Anthropologist.
Geertz, C. 1963. Agricultural Involution. University of Chicago Press, Berkeley.
Gerard, J.G., "Observations on the Spiti Valley and the Adjacent Countries within
the Himalayas," Asiatic Researches, XVIII, 1933.
Gill, Manohar Singh, Himalayan Wonderland: Travel in Lahaul Spiti (Delhi, 1972).
Glick, T.F. 1970. Irrigation and Society in Medieval Valencia, Harvard University
Press, Cambridge.
Gluckman, Max 163 Order and Rebellion in Triabla Africa. New York: Free Press.
Goodenough, Ward H. 1964 Cultural Anthropology and Linguistics. Pages 36-39 in
Dell H. Hymes (editor), Language in Culture and Society: A Reader in Linguistics and Anthropology. New York: Harrper.

Grader, C.J. 1960. The irrigation system in the region of Jembrana. In Swellengrebel, J.L. (ed.), Bali: Life, Thought and Ritual, The Hague and Bandung.
Grigson, W. V. 1938. The Maria Gonds of Bastar, Bombay, Oxford University Press.
Hagen, Everett E., 1962. On the Theory of Social Change, Homewood, III., Dorsey.
245
Haigh, M. 1984. Deforestation and disaster in northern India. Land Use Policy, July
1984.
Hamilton, L. S. 1985. Towards clarifying the appropriate mandate in forestry for
watershed rehabilitation and management. in Strategies, Approaches, and Systems in Integrated Watershed Management. FAO Conservation Guide 14, Rome.
Harcourt, A.F.E., The Himalayan District of Kooloo, Lahaul and Spiti (Lahore, 1874).
Harcourt, A.F.E., Gazetteer of the Kangra District, Vol.II, Kulu, Lahaul and Spiti
(Lahore, 1883-1884).
Hawley, Amos, 1944. Ecology and human ecology, Social Forces, 22.
Hawley, A. 1950. Human Ecology. New York, Ronald Press.
Helm, June, 1962. The ecological approach in anthropology, The American Journal
of Sociology, 67.
Himachal Pradesh, Directorate of Economics and Statistics, An Evaluation Study of
Lahaul-Spiti, 1974 (Simla, 1974.
Himachal Pradesh, Directorate of Economics and Statistics, Review of Achievements
of Lahaul and Spiti District (1969-70) (Simla, 1971).
Himachal Pradesh, Planning Department, Sub-Plan for Tribal Belt 1974-1977 (Simla).
Himachal Pradesh Government, Department of Agriculture, Intensive Agriculture
Development· Project, Lahaul and Spiti District.
Holmes, Peter, Mountains and Monasteries (London, 1958).

246
Holmes, Peter E. 11 Spiti, 11 Asiatic Journal, LX 1956 and LXI, 1957.
Romans, Goerge, C., 1941. Anxiety and ritual: The theories of Malinowski and Radcliffe-Brown, American Anthropologist, 43.
Hymes, Dell. H. (editor) 1964 Language in Culture and Society: A Reader in Linguistics and Anthropology New York: Raper.
Ingold, Tim, 1979. Social and Ecological Relations of Culture bearing Organism: An
Essay in Evolutionary Dynamics, in Social and Ecological Systems. Ed. Philip
Burnham and Roy F. Ellen, Academic Press, London.
K. Angrup Lahauli, IILahaul Spiti Tatha Kinnaur ke Bauddha Viharon Ke Vividh
Roop Aur Unka Sanskritik Yogdha, 11 Somsi, vol.2, 3 July, 1976.
K. Angrup Lahauli, II Lahaul Ki Lokoktiyan: Prayog Evam Prasang, II Somsi, vol.3,
4 October 1977.
Karmacharya, J. L., 1983. Planning the water resource development. Water Resources
Development in Ncpal. Thc Ncpal Digcst.
Khosla, Romi, Buddhist Monasteries in the Western Himalayas (Nepal, 1979).
Khosla, G.D., Himalayan Circuit (London, 1956).
Kluckhohn, Clyde 1949 Mirror for Man: The Relation of Anthropology to Modem
Life. New York: McGrw HilL
Kroeber, Alfred L. 1944 Configurations of Culture Growth, Berkeley: Univ. of California Press
Kroeber, A., 1939. Cultural and Natural Areas of North America, Berkeley, University of California.
247
Kroeber, A. L. 1963. Anthropology: Cultural Patterns and process, First Harbinger
Book Edition, Harcourt, Brace and World Inc., New York.
Kroeber, Alfred L. 1963 An Anthropologist Looks at History. Berkeley: Univ. of
California Press.
Kroeber, Alfred L: and Parsons, Talcott 1958. The Concepts of Culture and of Social

_ Syste,. American Sociological Review.
Kumar, L.W. 1978. Economic evaluation ofmicrohydel projects in hill areas. Indian
Journal of Power and River Valley Development, 28(7) ..
Leach, E. R., 1954. Political Systems of Highland Burma, Boston, Beacon.
Lethbridge, J.S., "Spiti and Rupshu," Canadian Geographical Journal (Ottawa), VIII, February 1938.
Lewis and Barrouw, 1956. Caste and Jajmani System is a North Indian Village,
Scientific Monthly 83(2).
Linton, Robert, 1955. The Tree of Culture. New York, Knopf.
Linton, Ralph 1936 The Study of Man: An Introduction. New York: Appleton.
Lowie, Robert H. 1917. Culture and Ethnology: New York, Boni and LiverighL
Lyall, J.B., Report of the Land Revenue Settlement of the Kangra Punjab, 1865-1872
(Lahore, 1875).
Malinowski, Bronislau, 1948. Magic Science and Religion and Other Essays. Boston
Beacon.
Mamgain, M.D. (ed.) Himachal Pradesh District Gazetteer: Lahaul & Spiti (Simla,
1976).
248
Mandelbaum, David D. 1972. Society in India, vol.I. Bombay, Popular Prakashan.
Manlinowski, Bronislaw 1960 Argonauts of the Western Pacific: An Account of
Native Enterprise and Adventure in the Archipelagoes of Melanesian New
Guinea. London School of Economics and Political Science Studies, No. 65.
London: Routledge; New York; Dutton.
Maquet, Jacques, J. 1964 Objectivity in Anthropology Current Anthropology 5.
Marriott, McKim (editor) 1955 Village India: Studies in the Little Community. Univ.
of Chicago Press.
Mead, Margaret 1963: Socialization and Encu1turation Current Antropology 4.
Merton, Robert K., 1949. Social Theory and Social Structure. Glencoe, N.Y.,

Free
Press.
Murdock, Goerge P. 1932. The Science of Culture. American Anthropologist, New
Series 34.
Murdock, George P. 1949 Social Structure. New York Macmillan.
Murthy, Y.K. 1981. Water resources potential of the Himalaya. In J.S. Lal (ed.), The Himalaya: Aspects of Change, Oxford University Press, Delhi.
Myers, N. 1986. Environmental repercussions of deforestation in the Himalayas.
Journal of World Forest Resource Management, 2.
Odum, Eugene P., 1959. Fundamentals of Ecology, 2nd ed. Philadelphia, Saunders.
Parsons, Talcott 1951 The social System, Glencoe III: Free Press.
Punjab District Census Handboo: Lahaul and Spiti, 1961, Himachal Pradesh, District
Census Handbook, 1971, 1981, Lahaul and Spiti.
249

Printed by Libri Plureos GmbH in Hamburg,
Germany